Selected Poems

NICOLAS BOILEAU

TRANSLATED FROM THE FRENCH BY

BURTON RAFFEL

INTRODUCTION BY

JULIA PREST

Yale University Press/New Haven & London

Published with assistance from the foundation established in memory of
Philip Hamilton McMillan of the Class of 1894, Yale College.

Designed by Mary Valencia.
Set in Fournier MT type by Integrated Publishing Solutions.
Printed in the United States of America.

Library of Congress Cataloging-in-Publication Data
Boileau Despréaux, Nicolas, 1636–1711.
    [Selections. English 2007]
    Selected poems / Nicolas Boileau ; translated from the French by Burton
Raffel ; introduction by Julia Prest.
        p.   cm.
    Includes bibliographical references.
    ISBN-13: 978-0-300-10821-7 (clothbound : alk. paper)
    I. Raffel, Burton.   II. Title.
PQ1721.L8E7   2007
841'.1—dc22   2006026974

A catalogue record for this book is available from the British Library.

The paper in this book meets the guidelines for permanence and durability
of the Committee on Production Guidelines for Book Longevity
of the Council on Library Resources.

10 9 8 7 6 5 4 3 2 1

To the memory of Alexander Pope, a very great English poet whose praise led me to Boileau

Contents

Introduction *A Classicist in Modern Times* by Julia Prest

There are many good reasons to read and enjoy Boileau's poetry. Let us begin with three: first, his work offers an excellent means to understanding the precepts of French Classicism, a movement of which he is often thought to be France's most important representative; second, his *Art poétique* (the focus of the present collection) is the most important example of literary theory from the golden age of French literature; and third, his poetry is charming and accomplished in its own right. Unfortunately, however, there are also reasons why Boileau does not appeal immediately to modern audiences as much as his merit and interest would warrant: he is a complex and subtle writer who demands that his reader should work to understand his many nuances. This can be a particularly daunting prospect for the modern reader of poetry who is not familiar with the climate of late-seventeenth-century France. But those who take up this challenge are rewarded with an appreciation of Boileau's delightful and intricate verse, the work of one of the sharpest wits of his time. My purpose here is to guide the modern reader toward an appreciation of Boileau on his own terms in order to judge him by the standards of his day. In the course of this journey back to the reign of Louis XIV, I hope that Boileau's relevance to the twenty-first century will become apparent.

Since the Romantic era, we have come to expect poetry (of the nonexperimental variety at least) to be lyrical, confessional, and highly emotional. Similarly, in our postmodern world, we distrust any form of dogmatism and our instinct is to reject anything that smacks of universalism. Boileau's views on the rights and wrongs of literary composition and his highly moralistic tone, then, can seem distasteful to modern readers. But Boileau is very much a man of his time, and it is important to avoid anachronistic interpretations of his work and to remember that his views were widely and sincerely held by some of the most important literary figures ever to have lived. Moreover, certain aspects of Boileau's poetry (notably his emphasis on audience response) will emerge as being in striking agreement with current trends in literary criticism. In our consideration of Boileau, we would do well to embrace the most important principle of his writing: the combination of pleasure and instruction. The content of Boileau's poetry will teach us much about Louis XIV's France at the same time that its form will please us. Conversely, we should also hope to learn from Boileau's poetic form and to derive pleasure from its content.

Nicolas Boileau-Despréaux (1636–1711) was an almost exact contemporary of France's most famous king, Louis XIV (1638–1715). Born in Paris into a legal family, Boileau trained as a lawyer, but his inheritance following his father's death in 1657 permitted him to abandon a legal career and pursue his true calling: literature. Boileau has often been portrayed as a frosty figure or as an angry, embittered man (he was reputedly the model for Molière's Alceste in *Le Misanthrope*), but this assessment of him is inadequate. During his youth, Boileau frequented bohemian and even libertine circles, and he included among his lasting friends both Molière and Jean La Fontaine. Throughout his life he maintained friendships with people from a range of backgrounds and of a variety of persuasions, a fact that suggests a degree of flexibility and affability on his part. Rather, Boileau's formidable reputation stems principally from his sharp satirical bent (which earned him many enemies), compounded by his enthusiastic espousal of the seemingly rigid doctrines of French Classicism. Boileau began his literary career as a satirist, and this aspect of his personal temperament and literary inclination remained with him (if later in a more muted form) throughout his life.

Having established a reputation as a talented and redoubtable satirist in the 1660s, Boileau turned his attention to literary criticism, adopting a more theoretical approach in his writing. With the composition and publication of his *Art poétique* in the early 1670s, he set himself up as the foremost literary critic of his time. The year 1677 marked a turning point in Boileau's career and that of his lifelong closest friend, Jean Racine. Racine's great masterpiece, *Phèdre* (1677), had come under attack from the playwright's jealous rivals, and both Boileau and Racine were suspected of having written a scandalous sonnet mocking two important aristocrats at the French court. Boileau and Racine were eventually absolved from this controversy. Not only that: that very year they were together appointed royal historiographers in recognition of their literary and moral merits. No longer mere writers, Racine and Boileau now formed an integral part of the Sun King's court: they accompanied Louis XIV on his military campaigns and were entrusted with the important task of providing official accounts of his exploits. In other words, they had become part of the king's famously elaborate propaganda machine. As it turns out, this type of history writing did not sit comfortably with either Racine or Boileau, though the official recognition from the king (and the generous pension that accompanied it) was certainly pleasing to both of them. It is no doubt partly because of this royal recognition that Boileau was elected to the Académie Française in 1684.

Boileau's late career is bound up with the famous Quarrel of the Ancients and Moderns, during which many of the leading cultural lights of the day debated the respective merits of ancient and modern literature and culture. In a dispute that turned on the possibility of progress, Boileau famously championed the cause of the ancients after his indignation had been aroused by Charles Perrault's reading of his overtly modern poem *Le Siècle de Louis XIV* (The age of

Louis XIV) at the Académie Française in 1687. This aspect of Boileau's life and thought, too, however, has sometimes been misunderstood. As chief representative of the ancients, Boileau is all too easily perceived as an old-fashioned stick-in-the-mud, but the truth is far more interesting and complex. First, Boileau was himself a modern author, and his decision to become a writer demonstrates a sincerely held belief in the merits and possibilities of legitimate modern writing. Further, he was a staunch defender of several major modern writers when they came under attack, including Molière and, as we have seen, Racine. It is emphatically not the case, then, that Boileau rejected all modern writing on principle—indeed, his writing career was dedicated to the possibility of the production of high-quality writing by modern authors. Rather, in addition to his engagement with modern writers, Boileau *also* defended the work of their eminent predecessors. And even Boileau was not indiscriminate in his support of ancient literature: he considered only those ancients whose work had survived to please posterity to be worthy of our attention. In the same way, he believed in the merit of those moderns whose work would continue to be appreciated in centuries to come. Given the importance ascribed by Boileau to the judgment of future generations, it is all the more remarkable that he was so strikingly perceptive in this regard: with few exceptions, the authors whose work he praised (notably Molière, Racine, Pierre Corneille, La Fontaine, and Blaise Pascal) have become canonical, and those whose work he derided are no longer considered worthy of critical attention. Clearly, Boileau was endowed with a gift for evaluating the canonical possibilities of contemporary literature, and his assessments continue to speak to us today.

Whereas audiences of the twenty-first century, as Boileau predicted, have little difficulty enjoying the works of Racine and Molière, it is perhaps harder for us to appreciate the nature and merit of what is now known as French Classicism. For some critics, Boileau came closer than any other writer both to exemplifying and to expounding classical doctrine. And certainly our appreciation of both Boileau's style and his subject is dependent on our appreciation of French Classicism. Even during its heyday, however, the principles of Classicism could never be distilled into a coherent doctrine, and the concept remains somewhat slippery. It may be helpful to think of French Classicism as a movement in the purest sense of the term: like a powerful river, it flowed over many decades, seemingly consistent to the casual observer but constantly changing in its details. Before we look at some of the principal tenets of French Classicism we should note the environment in which it flourished. French Classicism as Boileau embraced it has less to do with any rediscovery of ancient texts (a phenomenon more closely associated with the sixteenth century) than with the rise of an absolutist, centralized regime in seventeenth-century France. Under Louis XIII and his prime minister, Cardinal Richelieu, the Académie Française was established in 1635 as the official arbiter of national linguistic and literary affairs. Under its influence, French writers and critics were encouraged to be dogmatic, for it was widely believed that the rules of good writing could and should be defined for posterity and that this was somehow a matter of state. In our examination of Boileau's *Art poétique*, we would do well to bear this in mind.

In terms of ideas, Boileau contributed little that was new to the classical movement, and it is to those central ideas adopted by Boileau that we now turn. As its label suggests, French Classicism inherited a good deal from the writers of ancient Greece and Rome. Rather than simply copying the work of their esteemed predecessors, however, French classical writers were expected to appeal to a seventeenth-century audience by similar means and to achieve similar results. If successful, their work would attract readers through the centuries and become models for future generations of writers. According to classical precepts, good literature was expected to be pleasing and enjoyable to read but also instructive. The didactic function of literature bound it closely with a sense of morality, and it is in the context of this moral literary perspective that some of French Classicism's more opaque terms should be understood. Most of us learn at some point that French writers of the seventeenth century were expected to follow the precepts of *bienséance* and *vraisemblance,* but the meaning and application of those terms often remain obscure. *Vraisemblance* and the *vraisemblable* designate not simply that which is probable or truthful but, more intriguingly, that which corresponds to an *idealized* probability. Similarly, *bienséance* and the *bienséant* are often explained simply as principles that led to the banishment of sex and violence from the classical stage. In addition to a desire not to offend the audience with the spectacle of unseemly behavior, *bienséance* has a self-referential aspect that brings it close to *vraisemblance:* characters should behave as the audience would expect them to. The equally problematic principles of *nature* (nature or naturalness) and of *raison* (reason or reasonableness) should also be applied in this sincere but complex quest for truth and goodness in literature.

In addition to imitation of the ancients, verisimilitude, propriety, and reason, writers were expected to draw on their good taste and natural instinct for good writing. Even at a time of dogmatism, however, good taste proved notoriously difficult to pin down. Given the subjective bent of so many of these precepts, then, it is not surprising that even the writers of the time did not always agree on their precise meaning or application. Part of the richness of seventeenth-century debate (and Boileau's contributions to it) is precisely its lively discussion of these ideas, which turn out to be far more open to interpretation and far less prescriptive than they first appear. Boileau, then, could go only so far in his recommendations for good writing: ultimately, the quality of a literary work depended not on any rules or conventions (which anyone could follow) but on inspiration, on genius, on the *je ne sais quoi* (which was available only to the few).

Almost all of Boileau's poetry, including his *Art poétique*, is written in regular twelve-syllable lines known as alexandrines. The alexandrine was the preferred meter of French poetry between the sixteenth and nineteenth centuries, though it is most closely associated with classical poetry (and in particular with the tragedies of Racine). Before we examine Boileau's masterpiece, however, we should think generally about how best to broach his oeuvre and mention some of his other poetry. First, we should not (as many have done) adopt an excessively solemn approach to Boileau's work. Although it is true that he was deeply earnest in his attitude toward literary composition and that he considered the function of literature to be very serious indeed, Boileau's first principle was to please his audience. Unless he or she takes pleasure in a poem, the reader or listener will never take on board any didactic message contained within, and Boileau might as well write a moral treatise. And even in this moral context, it was widely held that good poetry had a quasi-moral duty to please. Moreover, Boileau himself clearly took pleasure in the creative process and enjoyed playing with language. An expectation of enjoyment will make us more receptive to, among other things, the humor that is a hallmark of Boileau's writing.

One of Boileau's favorite humoristic strategies is of course satire, and it is in his bold attacks on social types such as lawyers and moneymen or in his depiction of courtly and ecclesiastical vice that he is at his most accessible as well as his most harsh. In his comic and finely observed portraits of contemporary society we see Boileau's dual purpose at work: while we take pleasure in the wit and elegance of his writing, we are simultaneously reminded of our own defects as well as those of the people around us. Although Boileau saw himself as a truth-teller and as a scourge of hypocrisy, mediocrity, and pretentiousness, he largely avoided being too sermonizing in tone thanks to his fine sense of irony. As a writer, writing about writing, Boileau was keenly aware of the delicate position in which he had placed himself. This is apparent not only in the *Art poétique* but also, for instance, in his "Satire II," the opening poem of the present edition. Dedicated to Molière at a time when the playwright was embroiled in the controversy surrounding his comedy *L'École des femmes*, Boileau addresses in this piece the key question of rhyme. His moral and literary purpose is to promote the use of good rhyme in poetry. Boileau praises Molière for the ease with which he composes good rhymes and complains about other poets who are content with making simple, mediocre rhymes. Most interesting, though, is Boileau's first-person account of his difficulties as a rhymester and his purported envy of Molière's talent.

Although this is evidence of Boileau's self-deprecating tone, his comparison of his own talents with those of Molière may be disingenuous. Molière was certainly a gifted poet who wrote many of his plays in rhyming alexandrine verse, but his greatest talent was as a comic actor and playwright. Boileau, by contrast, was primarily a poet, and one who had both more time than Molière to polish his work and a greater investment in the nuance of every rhyme. This example highlights another aspect of Boileau's writing: it is often playful and sometimes deliberately ambiguous. Rather than attempting any definitive interpretation of his poetry, we may find it more productive simply to delight in Boileau's subtle paradoxes.

It is important, too, to remember that Boileau's poetry was originally intended to be read aloud at small salon-like gatherings. Contemporary accounts confirm that Boileau was an excellent reader of poetry who displayed a gift for mimicry. We can be confident, then, that there was nothing dreary about the early readings of his work. Although we may wish to stop short of re-creating a seventeenth-century salon, we should pay attention to the sounds of Boileau's words and the rhythms of his lines, a strong sense of which has been retained in Burton Raffel's translation. The image of Boileau performing his poetry before an audience is consistent with his lively, quasi-dramatic technique of taking his listeners to and fro, of guiding them toward one response and then surprising them with a new twist. With his personal approach (Boileau often appears in the first person in his poetry), his direct appeal to his audience, and his varied, polished style, Boileau's other poems delighted many of his contemporaries and offer much that will delight us.

Boileau's enduring reputation, however, rests chiefly on a single work. His *Art poétique* is the most complete account of his views on poetry and is widely regarded as the most important critical work of the time. Written partly in response to critics who accused Boileau of being too condemnatory and insufficiently constructive, the poem is loosely modeled on Horace's *Ars poetica* and heavily influenced by Aristotle's *Poetics* (which was first published in French in 1671). Aimed less at scholars than at educated amateurs, the *Art poétique* was intended to define a universal doctrine of poetry. Boileau began work on the poem in 1669 and gave readings of it in various states of completion from 1672 onward. In 1674 the work was finished and then published.

Boileau's *Art poétique* is a quest for truth rather than originality, and its governing principles are those identified above as being central to French Classicism. But Boileau also brings to the subject his unique approach and style, including his own examples of good and bad poetry. The work is divided into four cantos, unequal in length and quality. The second and third cantos, dealing with minor literary genres (including the eclogue, the elegy, the ode, and the sonnet) and major ones (epic, tragedy, and comedy), respectively, are in many respects the most accessible. They are largely descriptive and provide a valuable point of reference for anyone interested in questions of literary genre (though Boileau's account of French literary history is often inaccurate and should be treated with caution). For most readers, the third canto (by far the longest of the poem) is the more interesting of the two, for it deals with the two most important genres of the period, tragedy and comedy (as well as epic, a genre that is strikingly absent from the seventeenth-century French canon). In his discussion of tragedy, Boileau reminds us of a key paradox of the genre: deeply unpleasant experiences can be conveyed in a way that will give the audience pleasure if presented correctly. It is thus the duty of the tragic poet to ensure that the disagreeable is rendered agreeable through good writing. In his discussion of comedy, we notice that Boileau praises Molière for his more elevated comic writing but states that even Molière's work is inferior to that of his great Roman predecessor, Terence. This combination of references to both the ancients and the moderns is typical of Boileau's keen awareness of past and present, and emblematic of his preference for the ancients.

The most intriguing portions of the *Art poétique*, however, are its outer cantos, in which Boileau tackles the potential pitfalls of poetic writing and attempts to define some of the poet's more elusive endeavors. It is significant that the poem's opening lines remind the would-be writer of the difficulty inherent in this ambition. The reader learns from the outset that this is no straightforward handbook for writing poetry. Indeed, Boileau's poetics are as much a call to bad poets to stop writing as an incitement to talented poets to write well. Moreover, the nature of Boileau's theories is, as suggested above, such that certain aspects of them resist definition: How can a poet be certain that he possesses the *je ne sais quoi,* the intuitive genius necessary to set him above skillful mediocrity? Similarly, just how morally impeccable must a poet be in his private life to write good poetry? And to what extent can he conceal any personal moral failing by judicious use of his art? These are some of the questions implicit in Boileau's work, and the very fact that even Boileau ultimately leaves them unanswered is evidence of their fascinating complexity. The *Art poétique* ends not, as is usually stated, with praise of Louis XIV but rather with a final reference to the difficulties facing poets and to the corresponding difficulty of Boileau's own task of writing a good poem about writing good poetry.

Just as there is considerably more to Boileau's *Art poétique* than a rhymed list of rules, so there is much more to his oeuvre than nicely turned classical precepts. With his love of the ancients and his fondness for contemporary references, Boileau can appear remote to the modern reader. And he is certainly, as I have suggested, a product of his time. But Boileau's humor is timeless, and many of the questions raised in his work remain central to literary debates today. He may have arrived at different conclusions from those favored in our postmodern era, but issues regarding subjectivity and objectivity, the poet's relationship to his or her audience, the creation of the literary canon, and the relations between modern literature and its predecessors, for instance, are not about to be resolved any time soon. His poetry still has the capacity both to please us and to make us think again about the nature and purpose of literature, just as Boileau would have wished.

Further Reading

Remarkably little has been written in English about either Boileau or French Classicism, but the following books may be of interest.

Borgerhoff, E. B. O. *The Freedom of French Classicism*. Princeton, NJ: Princeton University Press, 1950.

Colton, Robert E. *Studies of Classical Influence on Boileau and La Fontaine*. Hildesheim: Georg Olms Verlag, 1996.

Corum, Robert T. *Reading Boileau: An Integrative Study of the Early "Satires."* West Lafayette, VA: Purdue University Press, 1998.

Pocock, Gordon. *Boileau and the Nature of Neo-Classicism*. Cambridge: Cambridge University Press, 1980.

Stone, Harriet. *The Classical Model: Literature and Knowledge in Seventeenth-Century France*. Ithaca, NY: Cornell University Press, 1996.

White, Julian Eugene. *Nicolas Boileau*. New York: Twayne, 1969.

Wright, Charles. *French Classicism*. Millwood, NY: Kraus, 1966.

Selected Poems

Satire II: To Monsieur de Molière

Oh famous mind, unique, which pours out lines
But never fights or frets for metered rhymes.
The Muse's gold comes flying to your hand,
Apollo's borrowed treasure, perfect-scanned.
Teach me, Molière, so deft in poet duels,   5
How versing masters dance, but keep the rules.
Your rhymes flood forth, I know, like milk and cream,
Gushing from your pen in liquid streams.
Digressions make no trouble, plots stay clear,
You cast your line, and form and sense cohere.   10
        But driven into scribbling (senseless whim),
Bent to rhyming, for unpunished sins,
I thrash, and bleat, and flog my fainting brain,
Digging words, pursuing rhymes—in vain.
From morn to dusk I plod the blurry verges,   15
I dream of *white*, but only *black* emerges.
I try to draw a knight, a gallant hero,
My rhyme-blocked pen depicts a hack like Puro.[1]
I long to praise some peerless, flawless poet,
My mind says Virgil, my rhyming word is "Quinault."[2]   20
No matter how I plan, or plan to plan,
Excesses push me on, my pen like Pan.
This drives me mad, I scream, I moan, I roar,

---

1. L'Abbé Michel de Pure (1634–1680). I have taken liberties with his name, as Boileau did with his character.
2. Philippe Quinault (1635–1688), dramatist, librettist, and son of a Paris baker.

My hangdog Muse indifferent, silent, bored.
Then, cursing Fiends who tempt an itching pen,   25
I swear a thousand oaths: oh, never again!
Condemn Apollo—all the Muses—cursing,
When suddenly I see such glorious verses
Spleen be damned, I flame immortal fire,
And once more tilting windmills, pant, aspire.   30
Forgetting useless vows, I stumble, run,
And bouncing line by line, I take what comes.
My tepid Muse enduring tepid music,
I offer well-worn rhyme; she won't refuse it.
I do what's always done, go picking here   35
And there, stitching rags from everywhere.
In praise of Phyllis, call up *high-flown miracles;*
Marvels found, at once, on *matchless pinnacles;*
I glorify a face as *bright as spheres,*
My mistress *shines eternal, has no peers,*   40
Dealing *burning suns* and *perfect wonders,*
Scribbling *sky-gold creatures, Jove's high thunders.*
Throwing splendid phrases, clouds of darts,
I dash off poems: no fuss, no pains, no art.
A hundred times transposing nouns and verbs,   45
My verse resembling chopped-up, stale Malherbe.[3]
But oh my trembling heart, which dreads the thought
Of words misplaced, and phrases dearly bought,
Panting hard at every rhymeless void

---

3. François de Malherbe (1555–1628), poetic reformer, advocate of clarity, regularity, and good sense.

Until my empty verses self-destroy! 50
I start, I stop, begin a dozen times,
And scribbling four, erase the first three lines.
        Damn the first wild fool who shaped this path
For turning sense to senseless, gold to brass,
Cramming words in narrow boxes—prisons!— 55
With rhyme to darken light, befuddle reason.
This deadly craft destroys my days; it smashes
Calm, impales delight, makes leisure ashes:
I'd sing, and laugh, and guzzle as I please,
As gay as any priest, as fat, at ease, 60
My days all peaceful, out of thought or care,
Sleeping well, then breathing placid air:
Unworried heart, exempt from burning passion,
Self-limiting, no doorway for ambition,
Fleeing fame and all its pushy friends, 65
Not stunned by royal riches, closed to ends
And means. I'd be so happy, envious Fate!
Just free me from this rhymester's crippled gait.
But yet, the moment madcap fancy rings
Its frenzied verses, black clouds fall, and cling, 70
And Demons, loathing gentle peace, fashion
Dreams of polished lines and perfect passion.
Helpless, trapped, I burn in inky rages,
Quarry fragments, rub out ill-starred pages,
And see my life quite ruined by sad-faced art, 75
I even envy Pelletier,[4] born to the part.

4. Pierre du Pelletier (?–1668), a poet more fecund than effective.

Oh happy Scuders,[5] blessed with fertile pens,
You spawn a book each month, for years on end,
You write, oh artless, pages drooping, dense,
Plainly shaped as if to spite good sense,   80
But books that sell (and some are even read),
Adored by merchants, praised by empty heads.
The rhymes go clank, in closing scraggly lines,
But no one cares, for see! it clearly rhymes.
You silly fools, enslaving art itself,   85
Try pulling Homer, Virgil off their shelves!
But scribbling idiots love their childish noise,
For what in sottish lines requires a choice?
They gape and labor, stunned, transfixed, amazed:
Did *I* write that? Oh wondrous, fabled page!   90
While noble spirits struggle, always fail
To capture perfect art (as truth entails),
Depressed to find what poor excuses words
Can be, displeased, yet pleasing all the world.
Their poems stuffed with spirit, still they take   95
No pleasure, wishing they could stop creating.
        And you, who see the depths my Muse can sink to,
Grant me grace, teach poems and Muse to think too:
Or else, since even help from you won't work,
Molière! oh teach me how to leave off verse.   100

---

5. Georges de Scudéry (1601–1667), proud, pompous, immensely prolific author of extrava-
gant works for the stage; his sister, Madeleine de Scudéry (1607–1701), in whose work he had
some significant share, was the author of long, sensational romantic novels.

To Climène

The world hurt me,
Climène, hour by hour.
I knew for certain
Love had shown its power.
Hearing the news,
You swore you'd never relent.
But oh, cruel muse,
It wasn't you I meant.

Quatrain on a Portrait of Rocinante, Don Quijote's Horse

This was the king of all good horses,
Flowering rose of Spanish steeds,
Who jogged up hills, and jogged down valleys,
And once, says the Book, ran—when forced to.

On My Older Brother, Member of the Académie Française, with Whom I'd Quarreled

My brother, yes, is a writer of first-rate fame,
      And a man of excellent parts,
Who's never shown the slightest regard
      For me. I think he deserves his eminent name;
His poetry's pleasant; his lectures surely eternal;
      But nothing in him is ever fraternal.

Epitaph for the Author's Mother

She herself speaks:
Wife to a husband gentle, plain, approving,
Whose constant sweetness proved him always loving,
Our speech was never mocking, biting.
Don't bother asking if our children inherit
      Such splendid spirit:
Just read these lines, and leave off writing.

Epigram: The Grateful Debtor

His world collapsed, I helped him survive.
I never saw a copper cent.
But even owing food and rent
And life itself, he smiled when he saw me.
How grateful he was, not to ignore me!

A Perpetual Student of Time

For thirty years (or was it forty?)
Lubin wound his watches, oiled
His clocks, polished glass and toiled
At washing hands and faces. Ought he,
Winding springs and rubbing wood,
Have learned a little something worth
The knowing? Oh yes. No one on earth
Told the time as well as he could.

Satire I

Damon—noble author, fertile Muse
That, year by year, played games with rustic views
And Court opinion—wore just burlap gowns,
In summer days no linen, in winter no down,
His dried-out body, hunger-stricken face   5
No better fed for all our empty praise.
Tired by verse that cost him time and money,
Cadging here and there, but earning nothing,
His closet empty, purse the same, in panic
Forced to flee from debtor's prison, frantic,   10
Far from cities, lawyers, courtiers, priests,
He hunted twin unknowns, viz. stillness, peace,
Rejecting hostile Justice, jealous Fate,
That sought to lock him deep in holes, awaiting
Death (or healthy snubs from fresh-faced poets,   15
Which wither faded bays before one knows it).
            Yet on the day he left, disheveled, pale,
Like Penitents in dismal Lent, he railed,
His eyes aflame and anger in his heart,
Distilling rage in valedictory art: 20
        "The Muses once lived well, in gracious France,
But spirit, talent, worth have lost their chance;
Poets, once so blessed, have now been cursed,
Virtue tossed from home, and hearth—and worse.
        "Let's hunt some cave, some lofty mountain rock,   25
That sheriffs, bailiffs, lawyers can't unlock.
Instead of Heaven plagued by helpless cries

Let's hide ourselves from vulgar insults, lies,
Still free, in spite of Fate and savage times,
Unbent by age and callous, casual crimes,   30
Not tottering, old and feeble, blind and gray,
Until at last Death sweeps us all away.
I've learned, so hear what counsel I can give:
In making France your home, know how to live
In France. So steal your millions, all in cash;   35
Starting nowhere, climb in noble fashion.
Old Jacquin[1] knew: his fatal fiscal lore
Destroyed our army swift as plagues, or war,
His profits piled so high that, written down,
They'd stuff a book all juicy, fat, and round.   40
For money rules this city, sets its rules.
But me, in Paris? Fool amid the fools!
Without a gift for cheating, lies, pretending,
Backbone far too stiff for violent bending.
I can't be cowed enough to let some proud   45
Rich rascal shame me: money talks that loud?
But scribbling flattering sonnets, sure to bore
The world? Selling self and poems to order?
My Muse remains too proud for stooping low.
I'm far too rustic, soul too hopeless, gross.   50
Whatever is, I have to call by name:

1. Jacquier, a banker who became high commissioner for military supplies. Arrested for em-
bezzlement in 1662, he spent two years in the Bastille; released for turning informant, he was
later fined 1,800,000 francs.

A cat's a cat, and Charles Rolet's[2] a shame.
I'm not much good at crafting verse seductions:
Adventure leads me off in plain directions.
Paris brings me sadness, left unknown   55
And poor, a body, not a soul—alone.
      "But why, you ask, such wild, such hopeless valor,
Poorhouse-aimed? You really love such squalor?
Wealth allows an honest upright pride,
But poor folk bend their backs, must scrape their hides.   60
And that's how writers, crushed by piled-up debt,
Can change the fate their cursèd stars have set,
And pedants, in this iron time, play jokes,
And turn themselves to peers, or royal dukes.
For Fortune plays its games on every virtue: 65
See them triumph, high above their birth-due,
Cruising Paris streets in gaudy coaches,
Decked like clowns, who once were crawling roaches,
Whipping once-proud France with savage laws,
Sucking blood, and flexing fearful claws.   70
They're dreaded—should be feared. If you dare dream
They've gone (and paid their taxes), watch the scheme:
They'll reappear before you know it, strutting
City streets, outrageous, powdered, puffing,
Plundering helpless Paris, armed, at war,   75
Offending even Heaven (as oft before).

2. Charles Rolet, parliamentary attorney, exiled and fined in 1681 (though later pardoned).

And old Colletet,[3] muddied to his rear-end,
Begs for bread (though no one wants to hear him),
A practiced bum, like many modish men
Lectured by Montmaur[4]—again—again.   80
       "Of course, our king, with hearty royal will,
Drops kindly smiles on poets, tries to fill
Their purses, mending worldly blindness, saving
Phoebus[5] from the breadline, poorhouse, grave.
One hopes too much, when kings can practice justice;   85
Maecenas gone, what good is Czar Augustus?
And these days, being just myself, what count
Or prince would bend his knees to drag me out?
Besides, how make my way through all the would-be
Starving poets—more than really could be—   90
Who push and crowd toward any open hand,
And steal the bounty from much better men,
Lazy, sterile hornets, flocks of drones
Robbing honey meant for bees alone.
Why struggle hard for over-touted laurels,   95
When muscles win them, never merit, morals?
Saint-Amant's[6] humor came from Heaven: France
Gave clothes and shoes, and left the rest to chance.
One bed, two chairs, were all he ever owned;

---

3. Guillaume Colletet (1598–1659), poet, member of the Academy, and poor.
4. Pierrre de Montmaur (1564–1650), professor of Greek and self-appointed custodian of morals.
5. That is, Phoebus Apollo.
6. Marc-Antoine de Girard de Saint-Amant (1594–1661), member of the Academy, an often Rabelaisian poet.

No gold, no silver, only sticks and stones. 100
And then! So weary, dragging door to door,
He pawned his nothing, went in search of more.
Head heaped with poems, teeming hot his brain,
He came to Court, and hoped for wealth and fame.
What happened, then, to this abused old Muse? 105
He crawled back home in shame, decayed, confused.
Hunger, fever ended courage, fame;
Starvation started, courtiers closed the game.
The Court's own poets were the height of fashion,
Now it's clowns and fools who always cash in; 110
No nobler spirit, art of defter pen,
Can rise like butlers, grooms, or scullery men.
     "What's needed now? Much different Muse-drawn roles?
Abandon art and ape the lawyers' souls?
Then black's the color—buckles, wigs, and gowns. 115
We'll dance in circles, slow and jurist rounds.
But just the thought bewilders blood and brain:
I'm lost, destroyed by violence so insane!
I see the pure go down those greedy maws,
Trapped in mazes, Daedalus wrapped in laws, 120
In whirled confusion, heaped-up legal cheating,
Black now white, both good and bad now fleeting,
And honest Patru[7] killed by lawyer sharks
(So fierce that even Cicero fears their bark).
My friends, before I go that route, the Seine 125

---

7. Olivier Patru (1604–1681), member of the Academy, son of an attorney and himself a lawyer.

Will freeze from Paris down to old Saint-Jean,
Jansen's[8] preachers flog the pope in Rome,
Sorlin[9] believe the truth, Pavin[10] go wrong.

    "Let's flee this pushing city, left behind,
Where Honor fights with Fortune, virtue's blind,   130
Where strutting Vices walk and talk like kings
(They hold up miters, crosses, wear gold rings),
Where learning's frightened, sad, without support.
We're hunted down like villains—noble sport!
The only art in fashion, here, is theft.   135
I choke . . . alas, I cannot say the rest.
But what unmoving man would not be moved
By Paris love? It's hate, and hates true love.
Oh how endure it? Once resolved, attack it,
Never mind Apollo! Kill it, smash it!   140
Don't strive for grace, on fatal fields like these!
Don't try for mighty art, when killing fleas.
Why summon beauty, fighting fiends and evil?
Anger's good enough to kill the Devil.

    "'Relax,' they say. 'Why get yourself upset?   145
Why fling great words? Talk soft, there's hope still left.
Go climb a chair, preach nice professor talk,
While listeners snore in peace, and let you squawk.

---

8. A morally austere movement within the Catholic Church, distinctly Calvinist in tone though
not in affiliation; Blaise Pascal (1623–1662) was Jansenism's most celebrated adherent, though
it made many converts among French intellectuals and artists.
9. Jean Desmarets de Saint Sorlin (1595–1676), member of the Academy, ill-disposed both to
Jansenists and to Boileau.
10. Denis Sanguin de Saint-Pavin (1595–1670), a cleric strong neither in conduct nor in faith.

Now that's the way to deal with wrong, and write.'
"They talk like that, who never want to fight!   150
They think they need no help, their lives are safe,
They like to sneer a poet in the face.
But weak-kneed men just play at being strong,
Who don't believe in God till things go wrong.
They weep in storms, they pray the angry sky,   155
But tempests done, they laugh at men who cry,
Assured that God will spin the earth around
And keep it balanced, hold it nicely bound.
Their lives ascend, surpassing any sin.
They won't admit the mess our world is in.   160
        "But even healthy, ah! that other world
Can make me tremble, shake at God's own word.
But where is God, if I am in this hell?
I'm going, gone: Farewell, Paris, farewell."

The Art of Poetry

Canto One

Rash writers, thinking verse an easy road,
Rush up Olympus toward the sacred grove—
Yet lacking Heaven's touch, its secret caul,
Not star-shaped poets from their birth, they crawl,
They languish, trapped in webs of subtle rules,   5
Phoebus[1] deaf, their magic steeds just mules.
      O you, your hearts consumed by licking flames,
Who start so gaily down those prickly lanes,
Don't waste your lives on worthless poems, don't think
Your taste for rhyming earns you nectared drink—   10
Fear empty pleasure like a mousetrap bait,
Weigh what you can and can't, don't fight with Fate.
      Nature draws on blessings rich and rare,
And guarantees each writer just a share:
This poet traces flickering bright affection;   15
That one's joy is sharpened swift reflection.
Malherbe[2] is fond of heroes, all their deeds;
Racan[3] delights in shepherds, Phyllis, sheep.
Be careful not to praise your poems too much:

1. Phoebus Apollo.
2. François de Malherbe (1555–1628), poetic reformer, advocate of clarity, regularity, and good sense.
3. Honorat de Bueil, Lord of Racan (1589–1670), childhood pupil and, in part, disciple of Malherbe.

Unwilling cripples still require their crutch.   20
Like Faret's[4] sometime friend (you know his name),[5]
Who scribbled poems on tavern windowpanes
(Which wasn't nice) and raised his haughty voice
To sing the ancient triumphs of the Jews.
He followed Moses over desert sands   25
And drowned, both he and Pharaoh, in those lands.
        Whatever theme—if pleasant or sublime—
Make sure that sense will always match the rhyme:
How often concord falters, jangles, fades,
Though meaning should be master, rhyme a slave.   30
So rack your brain, arrange the proper weight,
And sooner, later, rhyme accepts its fate,
Yoked by Reason, shooting at the mark,
And bringing Light, instead of dreary Dark.
Rhyme can blind a poet, boasting in secret,   35
Then pride goes toppling: see? he has no readers!
So cherish Reason: all your work should show
That glory, shine that light; the world will know.
        Yet poets, wildly pushed by far-fetched yearning,
Hunt for flaming sense, and words all burning,   40
Convinced they're shamed, their monstrous work condemned,
If other poets ever write like them.
But shun excess: let gay Italians prance

---

4. Nicolas Faret (1596–1646), member of the Academy, poet, and friend of fellow poet and Academy member Guillaume Colletet (1598–1659).
5. Marc-Antoine de Girard de Saint-Amant (1594–1661), member of the Academy, an often Rabelaisian poet.

Their crazy-quilted follies. Frenchmen dance.
Then bow to sense—remind yourself how tricky   45
Roads can get, how painful, hard, how slippery.
Poets quickly fall, and swiftly drown.
One path conducts to sense; one winds around.
        Some poets, target looming in their sights,
Cannot exhaust their theme, or get it right.   50
They see a palace, paint it stone by stone,
And pull us through, while rubbing feet to bone.
A staircase! Over there, a towering hall!
A golden carpet, fit for princely balls!
How many ceilings oval? Some are square.   55
"They're only scalloped blooms; they're not real pears."[6]
I skip ten pages, then another ten,
Nearly trapped on trips across the garden.
Use abundance like a poisoned pen,
Give up that game of poet detail-warden!   60
Lines you write too fully fall down flat;
The mind rejects them: much too gross—too fat.
Some details must be killed, some poets smothered.
        Yet flee one evil, help to make another.
Lines with middling sag get pulled too taut;   65
A line too brief may end up written short.
This line is not excessive, barely tries;
But *that*'s afraid of crawling, therefore flies.

6. The French—"Ce ne sont que festons, ce ne sont qu'astragales"—here necessarily trans-
lated somewhat freely, is quoted from Georges de Scudéry (1601–1667), proud, pompous, im-
mensely prolific author of extravagant works for the stage.

Desiring readers' love, and warm applause,
Poets change tone (as critics rewrite laws).   70
A style that never shifts, remains the same,
Glitters, gleams like gold, but still seems tame.
Thus poets born beneath dead boredom's star
Are rarely read. Who cares how right they are?
   The blessèd poet's lines are light as deer,   75
They shift from sad to soft, to smile severe.
Beloved by Heaven, prized by all, those books
Will leap from shelves like lambs from shepherds' crooks.
   However written, shun the false and showy—
Plain and simple poems are never lowly.   80
Avoid burlesque too brazen, which deceives
The casual eye, for gaudy leaves are pleasing.
But poems, today, are mired in vulgar rubbish;
Parnassus speaks like venders hawking garbage.
Rhyming freedoms need a firm-held rein: 85
Butterflies in costume flap in vain.
Though Paris leads the way, provincials follow,
Priests' and burghers' poems Parisian-hollow.
The dullest, feeblest craftsman wins his bays,
Even D'Assoucy[7] earning handsome praise.   90
This stuff will finally start to bore the Court,
These smooth and slicked-up poems that self-abort,
Falsely simple, heavy-footed clowning,

7. Charles Coypeau, Lord D'Assoucy (1604–1675), author of burlesques and a bad translation of Ovid.

In which the poor provincial ends by drowning.
Deny such dirty nonsense in your work!   95
Let's shape ourselves on Marot's[8] lyric words
And leave burlesque to poet-piggy sties.

      Avoid, as well, Brébeuf's[9] belabored sighs
At heaped-up Roman corpses laid by rivers,
And many mournful mountains quake a-quiver.   100
Write better, careful, straight, your reasoned art
Soaring, pleasant, never painted, hard.
Offer readers nothing bound to displease.
Audit verse for every cough and wheeze.
Make sure good sense controls your marching pace: 105
Caesuras (halfway through a line) can wait.
Watch out: for vowels that run a bit too fast
Can turn to boulder-blocks no poem can pass.
Words that fit together chime like music;
Sounds that clash get ugly, harsh, confusing.   110
The best-packed verse, the noblest thought, won't work,
But sink like lead when readers' ears are hurt.

      The Muse of France's early, unformed years,
Unschooled, unruly, roamed where flowers appeared,
Their words unweighed, their rhymes stuck on, appended,   115
Shapeless lines no knowing ear defended.[10]
All through those uncouth years our poets stumbled;

8. Clément Marot (1496–1544), Protestant poet, known equally for his light, witty verses and
for his translations of the Psalms.
9. Georges de Brébeuf (1618–1661), translator-adaptor of Lucan's *Pharsalia* (an epic on the
Caesar-Pompey civil war in Rome) and author of a burlesque of Virgil's *Aeneid*.
10. Françoise Escal, one of Boileau's Pléiade editors, remarks, at this point, "It is clear that

Villon untangled verse, and art was humbled.
Then Marot tended seeds and grew us ballads,
Constructed triolets, invented masques,   120
Forced rondelets to use refrains with rules,
And gave us rhyming lessons out of school.
And Ronsard[11] took those lessons even farther,
Adding brilliant paths that fanned our ardor.
His own career, bravura-glow defined,   125
Dug French from ancient Greek and Latin mines,
But those who followed tumbled back, declined,
And then pulled Ronsard off his lofty heights—
Yet, still, that proudest poet flamed so bright
His shadow dampened Desportes-Bertaut's[12] light.   130
Then came Malherbe,[13] the greatest France had known,
Insisting verse required an even tone:
He taught the power of regulated beauty,
And how the Muse would flourish, bound by duty.
This wisest poet quite perfected speech,   135
And placed it out of rough and awkward reach.
He taught our stanzas charming, graceful shapes,

Boileau, like others of his time, is quite mistaken: medieval poetry was governed by very strict rules" (Boileau, *Oeuvres complètes* [Paris: Gallimard, 1966], 991*n*20).

11. Pierre de Ronsard (1524–1585), poet and humanist, leader of the French Pléiade school, which included Joachim du Bellay (1522–1560) and drew on Jean Dorat (1508–1588), professor at the Collège de France.

12. Philippe Desportes (1546–1606) and Jean Bertaut (1552–1611), Pléiade disciples, primarily poets of love and religious faith.

13. François de Malherbe (1555–1628), poetic reformer, advocate of clarity, regularity, and good sense.

Discretely framed apart, demurely placed.
Then poets took his laws, this faithful guide
A model and a Moses, they his pride.   140
            Confess his rule, adore his purest spirit.
Directness shines: let all obscurants fear it!
Mark: if meaning's absent from your lines,
Readers wander off to nicer climes,
Promptly say farewell to pompous poems,   145
And leave their writers standing all alone.
Some darker souls, infused with blackened thoughts,
Beneath the dullest, darkest clouds must walk,
Where Reason's light has never yet shone through.
So think before you write; know what you do.   150
Ideas are more, or less, obscure, and each
Requires words that fit them, match their reach.
Ideas completely mastered fall in line,
The poet never needs to force a rhyme.
            Be humble, reverent; always write in awe.   155
Worship keeps your words from sounding raw.
For music by itself can't be enough:
Language needs precision, can't be rough.
Readers flinch at massive, pompous diction:
Inflated verse can't cure linguistic friction.   160
Opposed to language in his work, a writer,
Noble, proud, will never prove delightful.
            Don't rush yourself, whatever form you use.
Foolish hurry leaves your work confused.
Dashing verse that clatters out its rhymes   165
Will lose its force, and never turn divine.

Better brooks that slowly, barely flow,
That trickle past the flowers where they grow,
Than raging torrents, wasting all the land,
All wild and anxious for the muddy grand.   170
Make haste but slowly; never give up heart:
Perhaps the twelfth revision buffs your art.
Polish lines, and then again, again.
Add, subtract, let nothing bland remain.
    What good's a bit of sparkle, gorgeous, splendid,   175
When all the rest is sick with ills unmended?
What's set on pages must be where it needs to.
Beginning, end, and middle, all must cleave to
One another: poems of knit-up pieces
Lie like broken pots or smashed-up theses.   180
Keep your poem pointed where it's going,
Instead of searching clouds for words more glowing.
    You're worried people may not like your poems?
Become your critic, cast creative stones.
Stupidity admires itself, unbated.   185
The wise man lets his friends select what's hated.
Allow their honest love to tell your faults,
Assume the role of friendship's zealous force.
Stand forth, in front of them, without your pride.
Friends don't flatter: why should you go hide?   190
They'll praise you, when they can—but often tease:
Prefer advice to words that merely please.
    Fawning false-friends make a lot of noise,
They faint, they fall, they cry: "Divine! Oh glorious!
Charming! Perfect! Not a word offends."   195

They paw the ground, their weeping pleasure intense,
And pour out pails of praise upon your head.
Mere truth could not compete. But truth has fled.

      An honest friend is hard, he holds your hand
To fires, without delight, a stalwart man,   200
Excuses nothing, helps you see what's careless,
Makes you fix connections close and airless,
Expressions striving grandly toward the moon,
Or else too dense, too dull, too loose. "Just prune,"
He says. "Then tighten. Clarify." You do,   205
In gratitude for counsel spoken true.
What seems to him obscure, so seems to you.

      But often headstrong writers shun suggestions,
Fight with criticism, bark at questions.
Believe the best defense to be offensive.   210
Suppose you tell him, "Now, this word's unsavory"—
"That word," he says, "demands the reader's favor."
He's quick, you have no chance. "Now, *this* seems cold,
I'd take it out." "It fits the ideal mold!"
"This phrase rings false." "But all the world adores it!"   215
He contradicts his critics, word by word,
And labels every adverse point absurd.
Nothing you can say is ever heard.
Of course, he loves, he simply craves advice:
"Respectful, knowing comments have no price!"   220
This flattering, buzzing pretty-pretty screed
Is just a trick, to make you hear him read.
And when that's done, he leaves, so proud of verses
He's off to make some other ears rehearse them.

And oh he does! Our time is rich in fools   225
Who write, and fools who hear. They know no rules
And sprout up everywhere, in towns, in cities,
Duchies, farms, and palaces and privies.
Awful art is always welcomed, here:
It's loved, it's praised, admired—it's much revered.   230
Nothing's dull enough so fools won't like it,
Fools find fools to read, and fools to write it.

Canto Two

As lady shepherds, readied for a fair,
Will never pile up rubies in their hair,
Or deck themselves in gold or brilliant gems,
But pluck plain blooms from simple woodland stems,
So pastoral poems, if true to gentle Nature,   5
Are calm, relaxed, and free of pomp, of blather.
Instead of ostentatious, simple, pleasant;
In place of thunder, lines derived from peasants.
Sweetness charms, it's stirring, pleasing, clever,
Needing no fat words that shock you—never!   10
Yet sometimes rhymesters, backs against the wall,
Will bring in flutes, let furious oboes call,
And even, in their pompous indiscretion,
Break eclogues right in half, as trumpets beckon!
A frightening clamor: Pan will hide in roses,   15
And fearful nymphs conceal themselves in posies.
Still other poets droop so ghastly low
Their shepherds cluck like hens, like roosters crow.

Their vulgar poems, devoid of every pleasure,
Crawl dirty ground, in woeful, dismal leisure.   20
It's said that Ronsard, playing "rustic flutes,"
Would sit there, humming heavy peasant tunes,
Making Frenchmen out of Greeks, indifferent
To clashing consonants and vowels flat bent.

      The road between these two extremes is hard,   25
But Virgil's still a guide—most useful bard.
Theocritus as well, and Moschus, Bion:
The graceful verse we like to keep our eye on.
Such learned poems, as nothing else will, teach
Of lissome lines that never sag—or preach.   30
Sing Flora, orchards, shepherds, fields, Pomona.[14]
Bucolic, quarreling swains, and love's aroma.
Narcissus flowering, Daphne sprouting leaves,
Extol the amorous games that loving breeds,
And make the artful eclogue live again   35
For witty women and their martial men.
Pastoral poems can have this grace, this power.

      And elegies, not boastful, sing still louder,
But sadder, draped in flowing, thoughtful bays,
Hair disheveled, moaning over graves.   40
These poems depict love's sadness, praise its joys,
Cajole a mistress, please her, fight, annoy.
But just a poet's not enough for love
And all its wondrous whims, which need a lover.

14. Roman fruit-goddess, wife of Vertumnus.

Despise all writers pushing frozen zeal, 45
Who stuff their frigid lines with forced appeal,
Who offer chilling art, insane but calm,
Flog readers' ice-filled hearts with desperate balm.
Their sweet delights are empty, loveless words,
Forever blessing chains, and love's hard terms, 50
Adoring barren prison cells, and martyrs,
Hating Reason, wooing haughty Tartars.
This stupid stuff inspire a lovesick Roman?
Ovid stirred to write such tender poems on
Slop? His lines that ache with desperate sweetness? 55
He lived on failure, sang with love's completeness.
Elegies sing from hearts, and in hearts' voice.
        But odes must swagger, burst with potent joy,
And loft their brilliant phrases to the clouds,
Their verse enlightening gods, ambitious, proud. 60
They sing Olympic wrestlers, name by name,
Great dusty warriors wrapped in lasting fame.
They bring Achilles, bloody, toward the sea,
Show France subduing fiercest Germany,
Like bees that, busy under petals, buzz 65
The sweetness out of flowers' honeyed fuzz.
They picture banquets, dance with happy laughter,
Kiss maiden lips, and celebrate them after:
Attempting nonresistance, maids will frown,
Then yield, as barriers, lovers tumble down. 70
These pungent poems may seem quite out of breath,
But what may look like chaos acts like stealth.

How different timid jigglers, stiff and cold,
Whose artificial passions can't be bold—
Who rhyme a brilliant hero's robust steps   75
Like ticking clocks, till deafened readers sleep.
They drain their mighty potions sip by sip,
To make us suck each single drop of it.
They show exactly how the conquering king
Would ride his horse, and wear his diamond ring.   80
They barely keep Apollo's fire from nodding.

It's said that glorious, ancient, artful god,
Hoping soon to snuff these sniffling rhymers,
Parnassian pests, Olympian social climbers,
Invented sonnets, trusting complex laws   85
Of form and sense to give these fellows pause,
Sestet, octave, balanced on each other,
Song and substance tightly bound as brothers.
This poem gave no freedom, order ruled.
Apollo's hand designed its fearsome tools,   90
Forbidding feeble lines to walk his hall,
Or stuttering words to echo, wall to wall.
He shaped this dazzling form like godlike foam,
One perfect contour worth a thousand poems.
Though hordes of desperate scribblers tried to write it,   95
None succeeded, hacks were sad and frightened.
Read your Gombaut, Maynard, Malleville,[15]
And see if, out of hundreds, one's not vile.

15. Jean Ogier de Gombaut (1570–1666), François Maynard (1582–1646), and Claude de Malleville (1597–1647), all poets and original members of the Academy.

But who can read the rest, whoever wrote them?
Books don't come from grocers, or by the groat.   100
Alas! Like shoes that can't fit any feet,
These lines are framed too strong, or else too weak.
    But Epigrams are freer, unconfined,
Though often simply one or two good rhymes.
Our writers used to shun these jiggling jests,   105
And let Italians do their very best.
The lower classes, fond of frauds and pleasure,
Bolted tidbits, measure after measure,
Until appreciation swelled the tide
And poets thought their jokes were deified.   110
The Madrigal went under: that came first,
Then even swollen Sonnet-bubbles burst.
Though drama tried to vaunt its tragic gleams,
And Elegy spun webs of poignant dreams,
Heroes donned their most resplendent clothes,   115
And lovers scarcely dared to blow their noses,
Though shepherds, singing songs of rustic pain,
Performed like Muses, more than loving swains,
Words, like diamonds, dulled when double-cut,
So prose sneaked through the door that once was shut.   120
Our palace lawyers loaded up their styles,
And pulpit preachers flashed compelling wiles.
    Until, at last, offended Reason woke,
And said, "Enough of all these ludic folk!
Worthwhile writing can't be built on scandal.   125
But yet, the Epigram, though once a vandal,
Can still fit poems, if all its brilliant length

Gives off bright light, shows sense as well as strength."
And thus a huge disorder passed away,
And garish comics knew they'd had their day, 130
Insipid wits, inflated stale buffoons,
Whose poems were popped like overblown balloons.
A clever pen can sometimes, with a flick
Of the wrist, seduce a simple word to quick
And nicely witty trifles—but not too much! 135
A casual joke explodes, if heavily touched.
Push epigrams too hard, they're apt to bite
The hand that's fed them. Keep your jesting light.

      True poems can shine with faith, respect, and duty.
Born coarse, the rondeau found its way to beauty. 140
The ballad, bound by ancient rules and ways,
Does well in rhyme, in our more polished days.
The madrigal, both plain and noble, turn
By turn, breathes sweetness, then with passion burns.

      But fervent proof, instead of careless slander, 145
Is Satire's honest power, never pandered.
Lucilius, sworn to truth, first dared to show it,
Held mirrors up for Rome, made Romans know it,
Saving poor men's worth, not rich men's pride,
Damning rogues in coaches, pigs who ride. 150
Then Horace shaped this bitterness in play,
Rewarding fops and fools with dexterous pay,
And wreaking havoc where it seemed deserved,
He names the names that neatly fit his verse.
And Persius's poems, unclear but taut, drew blood, 155
Concerned with speaking truth, not daubing mud.

And Juvenal, when culture suffered shame,
Fought like Sampson for his Satire's name.
His work, so full of frightful, honest hate,
Made brilliant verse of stark corruption's state, 160
And scheming Sejan,[16] pushed down from his perch,
Both man and statue (both large bits of work),
And other fawning politician hacks,
Who ran from Rome to emperor, then ran back.
In painting nouveaux riches all drenched in muck, 165
Or Nero's raunchy empress (out of luck),
His lines flare off his pages, burning hot.
          Among these wise men's French disciples, not
A one but Régnier[17] truly knows his work,
Adorning Roman sense with novel verse; 170
Happy, making moral readers shun
The author, as they imitate his poem,
And much delighted when his slashing quips
Don't frighten ears not used to clubs and whips,
Since, after all, what Latin words can do 175
Is not allowed in French, so much more prudish.
Don't outrage censors with an impure thought,
Unless it's mollified with words more soft.
I try to keep my satire chaste, but honest,
Boldly moral, though in tone untarnished. 180
          A current song, not sly, just freshly minted,
Builds the French tradition, when it's printed,

16. That is, Sejanus: Boileau too docked the tails on names, when he had to.
17. Mathurin Régnier (1573–1613), easygoing man, rigorous moral satirist. A "hereditary" churchman, he had a reputation, probably undeserved, for dissolute behavior.

Nicely indiscreet, but swept along
From mouth to mouth, first strong, then growing stronger.   185
French freedom opens out across its poems,
Delighted dancing words that won't throw stones.
Beware, you jeering jesters, taking risks
With gross, disgusting gibes at God, who's quick
To anger. Throw your jolly atheist laughter
At Him, then go to Hell forever after.[18]   190
No artful poem, or poet, shuns good sense.
But luck and liquor, at their own expense,
Can furnish men with wanton, idle filth:
Consider Linière[19] and his grimy ilk.
If wandering vapors bring you such a bout,   195
Be careful other fools don't smoke you out,
For, often, authors of some prideful ditty
Believe themselves the genius of the city,
Refuse to sleep unless they've penned six sonnets,
Then rise with more, decanted from their bonnets,   200
Amazing, really, in their furry fury,
Printing up their poems for judge and jury.
What stunning portraits deck their wondrous books,
Since even Nanteuil[20] can't enhance their looks.

---

18. Françoise Escal quotes Claude Brossette's *Remarks* (1716): "Some years before the publication of this poem, a remarkably handsome young man, named Petit, was caught printing such godless, free-thinking poems. He was arrested, tried, and sentenced to be hanged and then burned, in spite of all the urgent appeals made in his favor" (Boileau, *Oeuvres complètes*, 996n1).
19. François Payot de Linière (1628–1704), poet, satirist, initially Boileau's friend and later his enemy.
20. Robert Nanteuil (1630–1678), famous pastel portraitist and (especially) engraver.

A slithering snake, a monstrous wriggling reptile
Drawn with art, will bring a happy smile.
Refined and well-schooled brushes thus create
Delightful objects out of things we hate.
And so, exactly, ancient drama freezes   5
Our blood. We weep for Oedipus; we're pleased.
So sad Orestes, cutting down his mother,
Makes us weep, yet eager for another.
     You who burn with fondness for the stage,
Now let your stately verse help actors rage.   10
Outspread your artful speeches far and wide,
And let all Paris watch you win the prize.
Yet who among you, given the most attention,
In twenty years will still deserve a mention?
You? Well, yes, if passion fills your lines,   15
Causing hearts to beat in rapid time.
For if no rapid trill of rippling passion,
Thrilling troubled hearts (in obverse fashion),
Won't mix its charming pity in our souls,
Then learnèd stagecraft's wasting time and roles.   20
No well-turned logic ever melts the torpor
Of lazy listeners, clapping hands on order:
They sleep as you heap rhetoric high and higher;
Awake, they burn your play in critical fires.
Please them, first, then stir them, then they're yours: 25
Their hearts respond to subtle feeling, not force.
     The curtain up, your opening lines prepare

The way for action. Substance counts: they care.
I laugh when actors drown in deep expression,
Rock-hard dull, so no one hears the question.   30
Struggling feebly with your callow plots,
They wind themselves in tangled, boring knots.
I smile with pleasure, clearly hearing names:
"I'm called Orestes—Agamemnon—James."
I hate it when the actors stagger past,   35
Unknown, confused, all bellowing like calves.
What's going on up there? Who knows? Who cares?
          Place *must* be fixed: who's going? coming? where?
Some poets toss their puppets high on peaks,
Then leap through years, as Time, protesting, squeaks.   40
The heroes of these bold, disgusting plays
Begin as babies, slide to tottering age.
But oh, the audience, bound by Reason's rules,
Observes these careless playwrights playing fools.
One place, one day, is space and time enough   45
To hold an audience still, a theater stuffed.
          Don't blind our eyes with unrealistic guff,
So even Truth can seem like boast-and-bluff.
Absurdities have neither grace nor charms:
Your words won't give that Venus marble arms,   50
And hearts won't pound in spite of doubting brains.
I credit clouds when wind produces rains.
A sober, sensate art provides us facts
That eyes and ears believe in, swift, untaxed.
          Disputes and quarrels, growing scene by scene,   55
Must boil to climax, quick, and sharp, and clean.

No pin can prick a plot's design as fast
As hiding information till the last,
Then flashing unexpected news that boils
Away the scenes through which the play has toiled.   60
          The Greeks began their stage with shaky steps;
A tragic choir, and dancers, did their best.
They chanted praise to Bacchus, god of wine,
And tried to please him, just at harvest time.
No prize was offered but a festive kid,   65
Won by Thespis, hung with leaves and figs.
Parading, stamping, laughing much like apes,
The world was joyous, leaping, drinking grapes,
As actors, scarcely costumed, stood in carts,
Amusing rustic folk with rustic art.   70
Then Aeschylus took actors from the chorus,
Gave them better masks, so not to bore us,
Elevated plays, for public viewing,
Let costumes show who's who, what each was doing.
And Sophocles let loose his soaring genius,   75
Adding grandeur, calm, subtracting meanness,
Giving chorus members pointed speeches,
Raising rough-hewn verse with smoother features
And making Greek-born drama nobly fine
(And, unlike Roman plays, of worth divine).   80
          Our pious fathers thought the theater low,
So stalwart France refused to let it grow.
Pilgrims, or a comic troupe or two,
Would pass through Paris, bring the stage in view,
Naively, still in piety immersed,   85

With Saints, and God, the Virgin, all in verse.
But knowledge slowly wore that farce away
And ended desecration in our plays.
Out went the preachers, speaking holy words,
And Hector, Helen, Troy, rose up in verse   90
—Except our actors dropped the ancient masks,
And violins assumed the choral tasks.

      Soon Love, so rich in tender passion's phrases,
Conquered drama (having prose pervaded).
Those who truly knew this lofty feeling   95
Stabbed the heart, and left the listener reeling.
Agreed: that road is right—so long as heroes
Love, and not disgusting shepherds. Dear, no!
Achilles can't be shown in love like Thyrsis:
Warriors must be warriors, grim and fierce,   100
Or else your Love, who fights remorse's battle,
Seems all weakness, better fit for cattle.

      Avoid what's petty, depicting noble men.
Heroic hearts are feeble, now and again.
Achilles could be nasty, furious, slow: 105
Let him weep at insults. They did, you know.
And grafting minor flaws on noble faces
Tells the truth, for flawed is what our race is.
May all our writing follow Nature's path,
And Agamemnon bellow, proud in wrath,   110
Aeneas still be oversolemn, stiff:
Let villains, heroes, be what each one is.
Study times and places, paint them truly,
For climate rots, makes sturdy men unruly.

Be careful (even novels sometimes can be)   115
Not to make Italians French, or dandies.
Don't hand your heroes sacred Roman names:
No Cato's foppish, Brutus can't be lame.
Romance prefers to fantasize its stories,
Well-pleased its plots amuse, not seeking glory.   120
Excessive rigor's not its first decision.
Yet theater asks a faithful, true precision:
Propriety's important, out on stage.

     But modern traits have just become the rage?
Be sure you show them in the flesh, devise   125
A path that lets them start and finish wise.

     Often, unaware, our writers paint
Themselves in every hero. Desperate taint!
Braggart authors make wild bragging plays,
Both kings and beggars sounding their own praise.   130
But Nature knows us better, banks our fires,
And every trait displays unique desires.
Anger's haughty, strives for grand expression,
Sad-faced heroes speak much milder versions.
Watching Troy burn down, its weeping queen   135
Won't rage and rant, displaying martial spleen,
Shouting maddened words in frantic phrases:
"A river floods our shore in seven places!"
Pompous heaps of high but useless words
Bespeak unknowing pens, and empty verse.   140
In sadness, men will drop their voices, weep:
He who's filled with sorrow dance? He creeps.
When actors fill their mouths with brassy noise,

The listener's heartbeats slow, untouched, annoyed.

       Plays in France must deal with picky critics, 145
Apt for spying out poetic sickness.
No playwright, here, swaggers to roaring praise:
Puckered lips will whistle off his bays.
An audience has the right to call us fools—
It's what they pay for, part of drama's rules. 150
And writers have to pay attention, soothing
All their critics, humble pie their pudding.
So write now high, now low, in pride, in passion,
First easy, later deep: just what they're asking!
Arouse them with your daring, startling turns, 155
Show wonder after wonder—flesh that burns!
Your language straight, not clumsy to recall,
So theaters keep your play on stage, and all
Your creditors are happy, calm, and mild.

       But writing epics asks a grander side: 160
Sustaining massive tales in mighty motion
Draws out plots, like salmon to the ocean.
Writers must employ their every art,
Embody virtue in an eye, a heart,
And then transform those bodies into gods, 165
Minerva, Venus, Zeus—the pagan squads.
It can't be clouds from which descend loud thunders:
Only Zeus can make such jagged wonders.
What sailors see as fearful waves and storms
Is merely Neptune in his angry forms. 170
Echo's not a sound in buzzing air,
But nymphly tears, bewailing love not there.

And on and on the poet wields his fictions,
Rolling out antique, archaic diction,
A painter dabbing colors with his pen,   175
Until, behold! the flowers bloom again.
Aeneas and his boats, new blown off course,
At Africa drop anchor, brought by force:
A common, ordinary venture, fraught
With Fate's rare passion, just as Virgil taught,   180
For Juno, acting out her godly hate,
Came up behind the fleet, and split the waves,
And Aeolus, the god of winds, then gusted
Far from Roman shores, as Juno wanted.
Old Neptune, then, came leaping out of water,   185
Calmed the air, restored the seas to order,
Freeing ships, released from godly bonds
—And *that*'s what catches readers, keeps them fond!
Without such decorations, epics die,
Or languish, moribund, as readers sigh,   190
Confronting poets, timid, faceless, shy,
Insipid weavers of a web of lies.
        A poet fools himself, but all in vain,
Ignoring decorations ripe with age,
Imagining that God and all the Saints   195
And prophets hatch straight from his steaming brain.
He only drops his readers into Hell,
Not even offering whiffs of Devilish smells.
No mysteries, solid truths of Christian faith,
Are paste and paper meant to waste in plays.   200
The Gospel teaches prayer and penance, guilt

And sin, not toys that epics stuff within.
To mix the blessèd truth and holy folk
With fables, spits on faith, makes God a joke.
   And what a sight to set out for the heathen!   205
Satan shouting insults up at Heaven,
Always fighting heroes for their glory,
Combating God like knights in ancient stories!
   Yet Tasso did it, some might say, and well.
He'll give me Heaven; I will give him Hell.   210
He has a reputation, even fame,
But time has brought no luster to his name.
His noble hero, always sprouting speeches,
Might have vanquished Satan, had he pleased,
Except he did his work with lovely women,   215
Dashing knights—the sort Romance will swim in.
   I make no case, in handling Christian themes,
For writers who indulge in pagan dreams.
I know profane and jesting pagan poems
Must lean on fables, not on hallowed bones—   220
Must grant the watery depths to ruling Tritons,
Show Pan deploying flutes, the Fates their bright bones,
And Charon poling, deadly shore to shore.
Shepherds were not kings, in days of yore.
Why pester art with useless, stupid scruples,   225
Whining, just like teachers courting pupils?
Before you know it, Wisdom must be banished,
And Titan Themis[21] holds no scales—all vanished!

21. Themis, goddess of justice.

Great Mars, the war god, looks with brassy stare,
And racing Time gets dressed in clockish wear.   230
No critic, wishing for a truthful story,
Strives to wipe out epic allegory.
Applaud the ancient world for what it was,
Don't try your soul with what the pagan does.
True Christians need no empty, silly fears   235
Of Agamemnon's sword or Priam's tears.
         Fables offer reams of healthy pleasure,
Their very names seem coined for cheerful leisure—
Orestes, Paris, Hector, Zeus, Odysseus,
Patroclus, Priam, Helen, Menelaeus.   240
Such riches must condemn the surly writer
Who names his hero Hildebrand. How frightful!
One harsh, unpleasant, jangling name or title
Can make bizarre what might have been delightful.
         You wish to curry favor, never lose it?   245
Choose worthy heroes, let your poem prove it.
Give us shining heroes, bold and brave!
Not perfect souls, but valiant, large, and famous,
Whose deeds are worth our hearing, noble, fine,
Like those of Caesar, Alexander's line—   250
Not Oedipus's sons, conceived in sin.
A tale must warm our hearts, to draw us in.
Too many high adventures soon seem endless:
Achilleus and anger, stark and friendless,
Furnished Homer with sufficient plot.   255
A heap of stories doesn't fill the pot.
         Display the action crisply, swift and sharp,

In stately words, evocative and barbed.
True elegance requires a poem to soar.
Events both low and vulgar leave us bored.   260
Don't imitate that fool, who painted gaping
Waves, in which a Hebrew slave escaped
From death by drowning, fleeing unjust masters,
As fishes watched his progress from their pastures.[22]
He also shows us babies "jumping up   265
And fetching pebbles for their mothers' cup,"
Thus fixing readers' eyes on useless sights.
O do thou better, when thou com'st to write!

      Start off in simple style, as things begin.
Don't mount on high, on magic steeds, or fins,   270
Shouting verse like thunder, fiercely hurled,
"I sing the conquering of our conquered world!"[23]
What more can writers offer, after that?
A mountain labors, out come mice and cats.
Oh how I love it, when they write like men,   275
Ignore Parnassian pomp, their simple pens
Explaining, calmly, how the story ran:
"I sing of warfare, and a pious man,
The first who crossed the Phrygian border, came
Through Asia Minor to Lavinia's plain."   280
No fires burn, no rockets fill the air,
He makes no claims, but treats the reader fair

---

22. As in Saint-Amant's *Moïse sauvé* (Moses saved, 1653). The next reference is also to Saint-Amant's work.
23. In Scudéry's *Alaric* (1654).

And shows him, soon, the sacred oracle
Proclaiming Roman fates, and miracles,
The darkness of Acheron, the teeming Styx   285
Where Latin emperors, deathly shadows, flit.
       Conjure hordes of fascinating faces;
Fill every line with pleasing forms and shapes.
No serious poet can be gay and cheerful?
Sublime events need not be dull and tearful!   290
Better Ariosto's comic tales
Than melancholy poets' frigid wails,
Starkly anxious not to walk at ease
While somber spirits feel the need to freeze.
       Majestic Homer loosened Love's own belt,[24]   295
Needing Nature's storytelling help.
His poem glitters, studded rich with pleasure,
His touch transforms the word to golden treasure.
Grace came flowing from his skillful hands,
His lines entrancing, never boring, bland,   300
A blissful warmth pervading every page,
A plot from which the poet never strayed,
His verse not bound to harsh, oppressive rules,
But all held taut with Nature's knowing tools,
Nowhere needing readers coaxed or warned,   305
Each narrative, all verses, subtly formed.
Admire this giant poet, love his poem,
And let its glories lead you toward your own.

---

24. See *Iliad* 14.214 ff.

A first-rate poem is unity sublime,
Nothing pushed by whims, or forced by rhyme. 310
But poems take time, and care: no callow schoolboy
Plays at epic art—a merry fool-toy!
Yet sometimes artless poets strike by chance
And accidentally make the Muses dance.
Sheer pride, and pride alone, puffs up their pens, 315
Creating epic gusts just now and then.
But stumbling lines can't march with crippled feet,
They jump, and fall, then roll, then gasp, then bleat,
Helpless, blind, all starved for verse's food:
Good sense, much reading, time, a gifted Muse. 320
If once these famished souls know printed solace,
Nothing stops them, picking public wallets;
They praise themselves, proclaim their meager genius,
Inhaling scents that sense would soon deny them.
They tell you Virgil's just a tired hack, 325
Homer's fashion's never coming back.
And if today ignores them, that's all right:
They'll find their praise as soon as all is night—
And while they're waiting, hoping darkness falls,
They'll throw up poems, like wildly bouncing balls, 330
Though no one buys or reads them, hid from sight,
Dusty, feeble, banished from the light.
But let them scribble hard, and praise each other:
They can't lead us astray; we won't be bothered.
      Remember: tragic plays were born in Athens, 335
The comic, too, was born of Grecian passion.
And Grecian wit: in playing pleasant jokes

They dug deep veins, attacking deadly yokes.
Buffoons? Oh yes, but joking for a cause,
Since wisdom, spirit, honor, shaped their laws.   340
The town acknowledged poets, giving pleasure,
And fed those poets from the common treasure.
One play showed Socrates unloved, unfeared,
But never, living, left to walk unjeered.[25]
In Greece, as here, that went a bit too far,   345
And playwrights found themselves before the bar.
Drama, courts declared, required sense,
And victims' names (or faces) couldn't be mentioned.
So theaters' crowing crowds developed taste,
With laughter framed in sense, not fierce or base,   350
No venom, rancor, tainted comic banter,
Innocence reborn in young Menander.
Whoever might be painted, out on stage,
Was watched with pleasure, not with jealous rage.
A miser chuckling at a miser's folly   355
Would never know it was himself he jollied.
Delightful fools, so perfectly depicted,
Yet unawares, all flaws quite unsuspected.
      Writers wanting fame from their light-fingered
Verse, must study Nature, learn its brightness.   360
Watching men, discovering beating hearts,
Will open treasure chests of passion's arts.
To know how monsters, misers, spendthrifts work,
And honest folk, and fools, makes food for verse.

25. Aristophanes, *The Clouds*.

Stretch a truthful canvas out for viewing,   365
And no one doubts your knowledge, or your doing.
But don't neglect a stream of simple stuff,
For human nature needs both smooth and rough.
The world presents us, rich and full, all colors,
Shades, and hues; each boasts its own allure.   370
A gesture, even less, can prove decisive,
Although some eyes can't see what's so incisive.

      All things must change, and time will shift our feelings.
One age will hate what others find revealing.
Young men, who bubble in their constant passion,   375
Learn love and loathing from the latest fashion.
Their speech as trifling as their wants are fickle,
They can't stand scolding: no one's quite so cyclic.

      Men grow riper when they age, learn wisdom,
Struggle up with all the caution in them,   380
Hope to hold our hammering Fate at bay,
Sure the Future never knows Today.

      Old age regrets accumulating pains,
Piles up for someone (not themselves) its gains.
Stepping through life at ever-slowing pace,   385
Condemning Now, adoring History's face,
No longer skilled at pleasure youth can splash in,
It what youth enjoys, until it's cashed in.

      Don't let your actors speak unless they need to,
Keep age and gender clear: be wise, take heed!   390
      Know the Court, but understand the world.
Plow all fields, for all enrich your verse.
At least, they may, discretely dug and seeded—

Advice our great Molière might well have heeded.
His doubly learnèd portraits, vivid, sharp, 395
Would often cut too deep for proper art,
The fine and subtle bent by angry craft,
Not shamed by staining poems with savage chaff.
This belly-heaving, overstuffed with clowns,
Pulled laughter up by dragging Molière down. 400
The comic fights with tears and sighs, prevails,
Denying tragedy its heartfelt wails.
The comic has its place—but not swept in
On dirty thoughts, on vulgar words and wings.
     And actors, oh! must jollify in style, 405
Dissolving tight-wound knots with easy smiles,
While plots march on with Reason for their guide,
Not wandering round as if they'd lost their minds.
What's sweet and humble makes for comprehension,
Showered down with witty, bold invention, 410
Bearing rich and finespun truthful feeling,
Well-connected scenes, most deftly reeled in.
Never mock good sense, to make a joke;
Let Nature rule the stage, obey its yoke.
Consider fathers, in old Roman plays, 415
Scolding reckless, lovesick children's daze,
And how these lessons strike at lovers' ears,
Who rush right out to do what fathers feared.
Not simple likenesses, oh no indeed,
But fathers, sons, and lovers, living, real. 420
     I wish for playwrights filling up our stage
With pleasant sense, instead of shocking rage,

Convinced their listeners will not hiss them down.
Away with writers pleasing all the town
With filth and falseness, foulness loud and coarse!   425
Stick them up on stage, on wooden horses,
Let them peddle stupid talk, and cheap,
To flunkies, beggars, shepherds, and their sheep.

Canto Four

In Florence, once, there lived a famed physician,
Learnèd quack, renowned for murderous mission.
He'd spent his years providing public pain
For new-made orphans, wanting fathers again,
For brothers mourning quickly poisoned brothers,   5
Drained of blood or dead of drugs—and others.
He'd turn a common cold to mortal fever,
Manage migraine into ruptured liver.
At last retired, rich and well, and hated,
One friend remained, one living, breathing patient,   10
Who gave our doctor gracious, grateful shelter.
His house was huge, his brain was helter-skelter,
But our physician fathomed walls and doors,
Profound in mansards, columns, tiles, and flooring.
A brand-new parlor earned his dry contempt;   15
A darkish hallway should have been a tent.
He liked a staircase of defective shape
His friend desired, and told the mason, "Make it."
The craftsman mended plans and built the steps—
In short, to tell the tale as fits it best,   20

The medical assassin changed careers,
Took square and ruler, left his poisoned years,
Abandoned fatal art, and human moans,
For setting roofs and walls, instead of bones.
        He represents a most inspiring model: 25
Be a mason, find the road to follow,
Work at useful trades that help your neighbor,
Instead of forcing bad poetic labor.
Most crafts have levels, some are high, some low:
Be second-rate, if that's the best you know.   30
But judging poems can offer no distinction:
Dull is bad is worse, until extinction.
A tepid poet means a hopeless writer:
Boyer, Pinchêne,[26] equal, unenlightening;
Who reads Rampale, bothers with Mesnardière?[27]   35
Is Magnon better? Corbin? La Morlière?
Crazy men can make us gay. We laugh.
But ghastly writers deaden with their gas.
Oh give me Bergerac,[28] who's pure burlesque,
Instead of Motin,[29] frozen, cold, and dead.   40

26. L'Abbé Claude Boyer (1618–1698), author—from 1646 to 1695—of innumerable mediocre tragedies and tragi-comedies; Étienne Martin de Pinchesne (1616–1701), poet, pedant, editor.
27. Jules Pilet de la Mesnardière (?–1663), a painter of richly artificial landscapes, published *Poésies* in 1656; his writing has only recently been rediscovered. Although Sylvain Monant identifies Rampale as an "auteur médiocre" (mediocre writer; *Boileau: Oeuvres,* ed. Sylvain Monant, vol. 2 [Paris: Garnier-Flammarion, 1969], 110), he seems to have been well regarded by his contemporaries; see Boileau, *Oeuvres complètes,* 1002n4.
28. Savinien de Cyrano de Bergerac (1619–1655), soldier, writer, mythologized by himself and, subsequently, by Rostand and others.
29. Pierre Motin (1566–1610), cabaret poet, known in his day for bawdy verse.

Don't let disgusting praise, applied like butter,
Shouted out by crowds, make hearts go flutter:
"Pure perfection! Wonder of our time!"
But recitation bolsters feeble lines
Which, printed out, all black across the page,   45
Can't hold the eye or satisfy the stage.
Disaster's struck a million would-be poets,
Printed, then ignored, so no one knows them.

      Weigh all critics' words, accept advice,
For even fools can criticize the wise.   50
Perhaps Apollo lent you sacred fire,
But don't inform the world of that inspiring.
Don't imitate erupting verse volcanoes,
Pushing up their readers' aching toes,
Taking sprinkled praise as true applause,   55
Pursuing listeners like a beast with claws.
No holy place, no altar, can protect
Against such raving, empty of all respect.

      Love your critics, guard them, take their help,
And let their reasoned protests make you well.   60
But never let a fool correct your verse.
A fool's improvements make the matter worse,
They wreck the whole, while aiming at the part.
For fools know nothing of organic art
And tend to argue from unsound foundations,   65
Rich in nonsense thought, and flawed creations.
Their piercing eyes can penetrate like hawks,
Although, once weighed, their seeing comes to naught.

Fear such counsel, make yourself a shield,
And dodge those dangers, meant to bleed you weak. 70
      Just choose advisers from the wise and good,
Who follow Reason's light through darkling woods,
Whose steady pens trawl slowly down the page,
Hunting error, lines all loose and frayed.
Confide your doubts, put trust in wise men's hands, 75
And let them ease away pure fear's demands.
Explain (they'll understand) how, here and there,
You've bent the rules, experimented, dared.
They'll help you reconcile tradition's force
With what the artist knows to be his course. 80
Such perfect critic minds are hardly the rule:
As judges of verse, poets can be quite foolish.
Famous for their verse, across our cities,
Yet men who can't tell poems from idle ditties.
      Oh writers, wise enough to heed my words, 85
Who want to please, amaze, with lasting verse,
Let knowing lessons guide your fertile pens,
And join what's pleasant with the good again.
The careful reader wants no empty claptrap,
Prefers a useful wit to clacking rattraps. 90
      The poet's soul, his manners, fill his poem,
Pervasive noble thoughts, and virtue's tone.
Rejecting honor changes useful writers
Into wolves, their treason seeming righteous,
Betraying honest men in public sheets, 95
Informing readers how they lie and cheat.

But poets need not shun the coarse and rough
(So Love reports them dull and tepid stuff):
No stage can lose such lovely, glowing wings,
That churn up brilliant tales and rich, ripe things.   100
The palest sweep of passion's honest touch
Renews our souls in shades of holiness.

When Dido weeps, her weeping charms exalt;
Admiring her, we still reject her faults.
A decent, modest writer won't corrupt   105
If virtue's real, no matter what's stirred up.

His heat won't kindle sordid-burning flames:
No evil fires flare when goodness reigns.
For Spirit, of itself, is far too weak,
Requiring Body, Senses, Heart, to speak.   110
But jealousy should always be avoided;
Vulgar, wicked madness works like poison.
Soaring poets need not fear infection:
Sublimity ensures complete protection,
Merit glitters right at rivals' eyes,   115
Who vainly hope to snatch away the prize,
Leaping high to show themselves the better,
Yapping dogs that can't escape their fetters.
Stooping down for cowards' vile intrigues
Is never useful: thieves form thieving leagues.   120

But poetry alone should never hold you.
Friends and faith and wisdom must enfold you.
How easy manners seem, as books are written!
Try living life, with living men and women.

Write for glory. Simple, sordid gain   125
Is nowhere linked to long and lasting fame.
Of course, a writer's work may sell, and earn,
But selling's not a poet's chief concern.
Some famous authors spit in Honor's face,
Exploiting glory and exalted place,   130
Allowing great Apollo workmen's wages,
Striving hard to peddle bargain pages.

      Before we understood the laws of Reason,
Men and women lived by work and season,
Rough and rustic, coarse, forever caught   135
In lives we know were brutal, hard, and short.
Force was basic, ruled all worlds, all men.
Murder stalked the land, unchecked, unspent.
But finally Reason, speaking harmony,
Softened savage hearts from sea to sea,   140
Drew scattered humans from their tangled groves,
Walled their cities, gave them towers, moats,
And tempered wildness with the power of laws,
So innocence could prosper, safe from force.
That harmony, we're told, was born of verse,   145
Creating myths and legends for the world.
Then Orpheus sang his sweeping mountain airs,
Taming even tigers in their lairs,
And Amphion's songs bewitched the very stones,
Which rose and made high Theban walls their homes.   150
That harmony gave birth to many wonders,
Sounding, here on earth, with godlike thunder.

And priestly voices, framing holy words,
Expressed Apollo's will in sacred verse.
Then Homer let the ancient heroes live,   155
And proved to men what honest courage gives.
And Hesiod, next, declared most useful lessons,
Displaying endless gifts, eternal blessings.
Wisdom worked in poems by the thousand,
Tracing out its treasures, spoken loud.   160
Hearts and minds and spirits felt its force,
Which entered through the ear, then ran its course.
The Muses, bearers of such happy gifts,
Were freely praised and everywhere were worshipped,
Altars raised and incense burned in shrines,   165
Celebrated near and far and wide.
But laziness and coarseness joined together,
Brought Parnassus down to jungle weather,
Focused love on gold-infected hearts,
And smeared decaying dreams on ruined art.   170
Yet worst of all, indulged the thin and pale,
Declaring poems—how quick, how cheap!—for sale.
          Don't blast yourself with such disgusting vice.
Before you yearn for gold, think once, think twice,
Then flee the sickly charm of total Licence: 175
Riches can't be drawn from wealth's cold vices.
The wisest writers, like the greatest warriors,
Seek rewards in fame and merit's laurels.
          But ah! a famished Muse, in desperate straits,
Can't live on smoke and glory, panting, faint.   180
A needy poet, stomach left unfed,

Oppressed by hunger, takes his need to bed.
Olympian satisfactions shun his door.
Horace drank his fill, in days of yore,
And never worried, like Colletet,[30] whether   185
Poems would bring him bread for that day's supper.
        Agreed. But then we know, in sober fact,
Our poets aren't often sorely taxed.
Today, these times and places, art does well,
And poets keep themselves in first-rate health.   190
How likely, really, given such rewards,
That hunger, deprivation go ignored?
        O Muses, shed your light on all who worship!
Choose your glory, not your grandest precepts.
Corneille,[31] who lit once more your splendid flames,   195
Deserved renown (like Horace), earned his bays.
Racine[32] created miracles on stage,
Devising heroes out of sacred rage.
And Benserade,[33] whose words graced Beauty's lips,
Was sung on pavements, cobblestones, and bricks.   200
Segrais,[34] whose poems enshrined the wildest forest,
Wielded epigrams and witty sonnets.
We have no second Virgil, no Aeneid,

30. Guillaume Colletet (1598–1659), poet, member of the Academy, and poor.
31. Pierre Corneille (1606–1684), dramatist; predecessor and rival of Racine.
32. Jean Racine (1639–1699), tragic playwright; the Shakespeare of the French stage.
33. Isaac de Benserade (1613–1691), poet, dramatist, and wit, who worked with the court composer Jean-Baptiste Lully (1632–1687).
34. Jean Regnauld de Segrais (1624–1701), poet, dramatist, and critic, who left the Church for literature.

Sung to strains of Rhenish-sweetened reeds,
No noble poet, climbing rocks and hills,   205
To praise the Alps, Batavia's fields and rills,
The storms of Europe, wars and marching troops,
Then dying, splendid, when his ship is lost.
Who'll tell the tale of Maastricht,[35] battlefield
Where Frenchmen chose to die before they'd yield?   210
              But who could sing that noble, grim campaign,
In which our armies earned eternal fame?
City after city fought, and fell,
And burned, defeated, like the fires of Hell.
Whose voice can sing the fearless legions drowned   215
When Dutchmen gave the sea their hard-won ground?
Fleeing from the French, but opening dikes,
Allowing ocean's waves to foam and strike.
What damage done! What cities, broke, destroyed!
What glory harvested, what fame enjoyed!   220
              And how to sing it? Let your voices rise,
Proclaiming courage, fearless wild surmise.
And even I, so used to Satire's bite
I never sang the trumpet's harsh delight,
I struggle, for this bloody, glorious fight,   225
To find some way of celebrating might,
And just as witty Horace sang of Rome,
I lift my voice in praise of France, and home.
Let passion push you on, inflame your heart,

---

35. Famous battle of the war in the Low Countries; France, defeated, was forced to recognize Dutch independence.

And raise your poem to high Parnassian art.   230
But don't forget, for all my martial fervor,
Poets' errors, in whatever oeuvre,
Must be spotted, fingered, brought to trial:
Error's claim to truth must meet denial.
I'm often a testy judge, right by the letter: 235
Why not be harsh to those who should know better?